MW01193897

Thank you for
standing together with
Connect Medical Clinic
Beth E. Chase

"Underground Fire is a must-read for anyone in leadership! The incredible illustration of a physical underground fire perfectly mirrors one that can burn in non-profit settings and the teaching points found within are invaluable as one walks through such an experience. The wisdom Beth Chase has shared is a true gift and will be a great help to many."

Christina Middleton, Executive Director, Life Resources
Duluth, GA

"Underground Fire outlines the issues and solutions surrounding internal meltdowns with organizations in a simple and practical way. I highly recommend it to all nonprofits."

Renee Wooten, former Nonprofit CEO
Vancouver, WA

"Underground Fire is a must read for anyone who runs a not-for-profit or small business. I wish I had this book years ago."

Susanne Metaxas, President, Avail
New York, NY

"Underground Fire equips leaders to survive organizational meltdowns with strength and dignity."

Penny Albarado, Former Nonprofit Executive
Jacksonville, FL

"Underground Fire offers a blueprint for leaders to mitigate the personal betrayals and vicious character assassinations that are common during organizational meltdowns. Every leader should have this book in their library."

DeAnn Visser, Former President/CEO, LaVie
Billings, MT

"Beth Chase brings a ground breaking, valuable conversation to the table in this easy to read, well written book. While the dynamic of the underground fire has applications to all manner of relationships, this book does an excellent job in bringing home the importance of understanding these principles in protecting the health and growth of an organization."

River Sussman, Executive Director, My Choices
Sequim, WA

Do you have an Underground Fire in your organization?

Find Out now!

Download the free Assessment

UNDERGROUNDFIREBOOK.COM/BOOK-ASSESSMENT

Underground Fire

Fire

Prevent, Identify and Survive
Organizational Meltdowns

Beth E. Chase

Prepared for publication by

www.40DayPublishing.com

Cover design by Jonna Feavel

www.40DayGraphics.com

Printed in the United States of America

Published by Chase Advancement Media

Disclaimer

The names and/or identities of any actual persons, whether living or deceased, have not been used in the anecdotes or elsewhere in this book. The anecdotes contained in this book are solely for illustrative purposes and do not portray any specific person or events.

This book contains ideas, opinions, and perceptions of the author. The author disclaims any and all responsibility for loss, risk, and/or liability, personal or otherwise, which may be incurred as a consequence, directly or indirect, of the use and/or application of any of the contents in this book. This book relates general information regarding organizational meltdowns and is intended to provide helpful information to those who lead faith-based nonprofit corporations. The author, publisher, and/or other persons associated with this book are not licensed attorneys. Nothing contained in this book is, nor should be deemed to be, legal advice. The reader should consult with an attorney prior to implementing any of the concepts or ideas in this book.

Although the author has made every effort to ensure that the information in this book was correct at press time, the author and publisher do not assume and hereby disclaim any liability to any person or entity for any loss, damage, or disruption caused by errors or omissions, whether such errors or omissions result from negligence, accident, or any other cause.

To all the leaders of nonprofit organizations who are making a difference in their community.

First, I thank my husband, Craig.
I am blessed to have you as my
husband, friend, and business
partner.

I thank Paul and Melanie Gibbs
for their invaluable contribution
to this book.

I thank my mother-in-law, Vivian
Arthur, for her prayers.
You provided the support that I
needed just when I needed it.

FOREWORD

Melanie Gibbs of Gibbs Consulting

Melanie Gibbs brings her background in psychology into this discussion of the impact that an internal meltdown may have on the mental, emotional, and psychological wellbeing of the leader.

Humans are made up of mind, body and spirit. The kind of intense and personal spiritual attack experienced in an underground fire can and will affect your physical and emotional well-being. Self-care is crucial for reducing the overall damage done to you as a leader, and for recovery after the fire if you wish to move forward unscathed.

One of the most personally damaging aspects of an underground fire is the ostracism inflicted by those you know well and have worked with for years. Suddenly the leader often finds herself on the outside of a formerly congenial and sometimes very tightknit group. Being an outcast of a social group (such as your workplace) leads to a loss of self-esteem and control, and may cause an increase in anxiety and depression. Physical well-being can also be affected by lack of sleep, development of ulcers, and suppression of the immune system. Anger and rage are often reported by those ostracized, making it more difficult to fight the underground fire with self-control and grace.

The leader under attack is often the first to recognize there is a problem, and even their closest coworkers may not see it. Rather than validation, they often are told by their superiors, executive team and other staff that it is all in their heads and that everything is fine. The shunning the leader may experience as the fire grows can similarly be 'crazy-making', as the leader feels they are unsupported and have no control over how they are treated. In more extreme cases, parties that start or perpetuate the fire resort to downright lies and denials! The result is similar to gas lighting, where the leader begins to doubt their own memories and perceptions about what has happened and may feel they are going crazy. This experience may be made more extreme if those on the attack are fellow Christians, using faith language and scripture to justify their actions.

What will help?

Acting decisively will help to regain a sense of control, however small. Every deliberate move you can make to fight the fire will help to regain the confidence needed to move forward. Maintaining relationships outside of the work environment is also crucial, and helps the leader to stay grounded in the fact that the ostracizing and crazy-making is isolated to the realm of the underground fire and is not a reflection on themselves.

Reaching out to others who have been through similar organizational fires can be very beneficial, both for building a supportive community where you can talk about what you are going through, and in showing that you are not crazy! So many others have been there and have made it through.

When self-care isn't enough

The leaders we have worked with have experienced this psychological stress at different levels and in different ways, shaking their self-confidence and sometimes even prompting despairing or suicidal thoughts. In addition to praying during the spiritual attack, resources such as support groups and professional counseling may be necessary.

Do not hesitate to seek professional counseling during or after an organizational fire. The stress experienced and trust broken can be very painful and may have lasting effects on your well-being and relationships. Remember, the enemy is trying to take you out as a leader- burnout, depression and anxiety are a very effective method. Seek help from a Christian counselor or psychologist if possible, since it is likely that others will overlook the spiritual aspect of this attack.

After the fire

Even if you have made it through the fire and are on the rebuilding end, or if you ended up leaving your position as a result, I strongly encourage you to take steps towards healing. That may take the form of talking with others who have gone through it, debriefing with supportive team members, journaling, counseling or more. The important thing is to talk about it! Avoiding, ignoring or 'stuffing' the experience will only prolong the stress, which could continue to impact your work and daily life.

CONTENTS

INTRODUCTION

What Is an Underground Fire?

"Finally, draw your strength from the Lord
and from his mighty power. Put on the
armor of God so that you may be able to
stand firm against the tactics of the devil.
For our struggle is not with flesh and blood
but with the principalities, with the powers,
with the world rulers of this present
darkness, with the evil spirits in the
heavens."

Ephesians 6:10-12

I didn't know what an underground wildfire was until I moved to a part of the country where seasonal fires were common. While living in this area for several years, I witnessed the devastating problems that underground fires could cause. We lived on a hill that overlooked a valley. One year, we saw some smoke on the other side of the valley, yet no flames were visible. When I asked other residents in the area about it, they said that there was an underground fire that had burned in the area for years and had surfaced occasionally. When the fire did surface, all attention was focused on putting it out to prevent it from spreading to trees and grass and threatening nearby homes. But so far, they haven't been able to extinguish the smoldering inferno below the surface.

An Unseen Danger

Underground fires are some of the most dangerous wildfires in nature, simply because they are difficult to track and to fight. Those fueled by coal seams deep in the earth can burn for decades and release noxious fumes, as in Pennsylvania's now deserted town of Centralia where a fire that started in 1962 continues to burn and release high amounts of carbon monoxide into the air. One fire, known as Burning Mountain, has burned for an estimated 6,000 years in New South Wales, Australia. Many wildfires spread quickly and undetected underground, as is common during the summer months where I live in Eastern Washington State. These fires brew underground, consuming roots, buried logs and other vegetation, and are very difficult to identify with nothing to expose it other than an occasional whiff of smoke.

Underground fires are especially dangerous for three reasons: they are difficult to recognize, very unpredictable, and the damage caused is often unseen. You cannot deal with a fire when you have no idea it exists. Even when you are aware of it, it can be challenging to assess the extent of it and where it will go next. Add to that invisible, potentially deadly gases and the possibility of sinkholes due to the burned content under the surface, and you have a truly dangerous situation. Perhaps most importantly, with the fire out of sight, there is a tendency to minimize the danger it poses.

Conflict Brewing

So, what do underground wildfires have to do with nonprofit organizations?

I have been working with a wide variety of mostly nonprofit organizations for over three decades in both risk and crisis management. The experience has allowed me to notice patterns that repeat themselves in all kinds of situations, especially those that threaten to impede the mission of the organization or to destroy it altogether.

I noticed one destructive pattern in particular about 15 years ago when in one year, there were 10 nonprofits I worked with going through the same organizational challenges that brought them off task from their mission and attacked the character of their leaders. All ten situations were so similar that it didn't take long to piece together a definite pattern that followed specific steps with alarming accuracy. The pattern was so consistent that I began to predict what would happen next with those organizations that were lagging a little behind the others, and it shocked these leaders when my predictions came true. After that, whenever an organization in crisis called me, I was able to ask just a few questions to determine what stage they were in. I could then predict with high probability what would happen next and instruct them on how to either prevent it or properly deal with it. I have found the patterns to be quite consistent and predictable.

These organizational crises seem to begin with inappropriate attempts at resolving conflict which at first festers below the surface. It is often ignited by one individual or perhaps several people who believe they have been wronged or offended in some way. Though in some twisted ways they may think they mean well, they begin to undermine the leader of the organization and build up a team of supporters to do the same. Momentum against the leader escalates, robbing energy from the organization. The mission of the organization is interrupted as all attention of the leader, board and often staff goes into dealing with the crisis. The most damaging aspect is that trust breaks down between the leader and the board of directors, staff or volunteers, and sometimes even donors and the community. Ultimately, either the organization's leader or those responsible for spreading the conflict have to leave in order for the organization to recover and get back on track. Some organizations either never fully recover or have to shut down altogether. This kind of organizational crisis can devastate the efficacy of the organization and its mission for good.

Spiritual Battle

As a Christian working almost primarily with Christian organizations and/or Christian leaders, it is impossible to ignore the spiritual aspects of this phenomenon. Any time you are working to further God's mission and bring good into the world, you will be opposed by the forces of darkness.

> "Therefore, put on the armor of God, that you may be able to resist on the evil day and, having done everything, to hold your ground."
>
> (Ephesians 6:13)

Every day, whether we work in the secular world or in Christian ministry, we are engaged in a war, not against human beings, but against the forces of darkness that wish to break down our faith and render our service ineffective. Recognizing the spiritual nature of this kind of crisis will help us to deal with it appropriately while not losing our faith in God or in people. It is especially important to keep in mind who our true enemy is throughout the battle. Although it feels like we can point directly to those in our organization that are leading the attack, they almost always mean well and are not aware that they are being used by the forces of darkness to distract and destroy. We are all fallible human beings and any of us can be used to do harm if we are not careful and do not seek God's wisdom.

Although incredibly rare, it is worth noting that occasionally, there may be someone in your organization that *does* intend to do harm. Though typically due to some sort of mental or spiritual affliction, such as a narcissistic personality, I have occasionally uncovered more unexpected reasons.

A particularly bizarre example comes from a board of an organization that had several members exit at the same time, leaving them with only three members. There was a feeling of desperation to increase the number of board members, and a woman stepped forward to apply for membership. In their rush (and I believe, their naiveté), no one checked on her references because everything looked good and she did attend a local church.

The group brought her on as a board member and it wasn't until about 9 months later that someone in the community alerted them that she was not who she said she was. Apparently in an attempt to enter a leadership role in her church, she had been exposed as a practicing witch and active in her local coven. Though the nonprofit had yet to feel the negative effects, the board confronted her and she admitted to having deliberately infiltrated their group. Even though they never learned this woman's motives, it was still an unnerving experience and a good example of the importance of knowing who you partner with. When you bring someone on the board, volunteer team or staff, you are entering a spiritual partnership with them. Scripture says a lot about partnerships. You take on their spiritual strengths but also their spiritual vulnerabilities.

Parallel Patterns

Over time, as I discerned a pattern to Underground Fires, I was able to break it down into four distinct stages, each with its own characteristics. In each stage, I noticed there were certain actions that would either help the leader move the organization past that stage, or would add fuel to the attack against him/her. I noticed that this pattern seemed to parallel underground fires in the natural world, and that this analogy provided a framework to better understand this organizational phenomenon. Underground fires always start in a hidden, unseen way before emerging and spreading quickly.

Just like underground wildfires, organizational underground fires are difficult to detect, assess, track and extinguish.

In the last 15 years, I have worked with over 100 nonprofit organizations that have experienced an underground fire and I have seen the devastation that results. I decided to write this book because I believe that understanding underground fires, recognizing the indicators and implementing preventative strategies will help organizations to prevent and extinguish underground fires thereby ensuring they are able to stay on mission. Underground fires can happen in any kind of business or organization, but my hope is that the insights provided in this book can help to decrease the frequency of fires by implementing steps of prevention, as well as drastically reduce the resulting damage of any internal crises that are unpreventable.

The Stages

Before I can present an overview of the four stages of an organizational underground fire, I would first like to refer readers to the book Necessary Endings by Dr. Henry Cloud. I recommend this book to every executive director that I coach because it is very beneficial in understanding and interacting effectively with the different kinds of people involved in the organization. This is so crucial in preventing and fighting underground fires as it impacts the communication style which is most effective and what outcomes you can expect from interactions with certain people. One section of the book concentrates on what Dr. Cloud defines as the three kinds of people you will encounter in the world: wise, foolish and evil people. Wise, foolish and evil people can each play a part in an organizational underground fire.

Hopefully, every person you deal with in your organization will be a wise person. This means they are willing to listen and take responsibility for their own mistakes rather than placing blame. Unfortunately, you are likely to encounter many people who do not match this description.

Unlike wise people who are usually a breeze to work with, a foolish person can be frustrating to deal with. For example, you may have to inform a foolish staff member time and time again that she must never approach a board member directly regarding a grievance issue without following the proper process outlined in the organization's grievance policy. But, being foolish as she is, she fails to change and continues her unruly behavior which then necessitates that a different approach be taken.

When repeated reminders have resulted in plenty of frustration but no change, the strategy for dealing with this person needs an adjustment to include consequences for her behavior or the particular behavior will never change. People who begin underground fires are often foolish people, and they usually find fellow foolish people to perpetuate the damage. Foolish people do not set out to cause damage but can be some of the most active and destructive contributors to underground fires.

Although rare, it is definitely possible to encounter an evil person involved in your organization. This label may sound harsh, but I would encourage you to read Dr. Cloud's Biblical basis for the labeling and traits of this categorization. An evil person is someone who is seeking destruction. This person may still want the best for the organization, but they believe that this includes destroying a person, an entire board or someone's reputation in the process. If you do encounter an evil person in your organization, follow Dr. Cloud's advice when it comes to dealing with them. Ideally have no direct contact with them; communicate only when necessary and only through your attorney. Seriously, you have to be wise and not underestimate the damage an evil person can do. Take my advice and that of Dr. Cloud; use your attorney.

With that in mind, let's migrate the discussion into the four stages of an organizational underground fire: Smoke, Flames, Firefighting and Aftermath.

CHAPTER ONE

Stage One: Smoke *(Something doesn't feel right.)*

Houston, we have a problem…

A friend of mine was the principle of a small parochial school. She had always had a great relationship with her staff and was able to laugh and joke with them on a regular basis. During a major transition for the school to a new style of curriculum, she began noticing a change in her staff. There was less laughter in the main office and people seemed to avoid eye contact in the hallways and at staff meetings. At one point, she walked into the staff room and a group of teachers abruptly stopped their conversation. She knew there was something brewing but didn't know how to proceed. Pretty soon, the school was in a large and destructive underground fire.

Smoke

In the dry forested areas of eastern Washington State, it is not unheard of to be walking along and smell just the hint of the odor of smoke or see a small puff of smoke from the ground seemingly without the presence of an actual fire. This is because the fire is burning below ground, consuming the tinder dry root systems of trees that have been dead for some time, probably years. Even though there may be small warning signs, it can be difficult or impossible to know exactly where the fire is, how far the damage may have spread or where it might emerge and kindle a roaring wildfire.

Dissatisfaction

Much like an actual physical underground fire, an organizational underground fire (dissatisfaction, hurt, offense, misunderstanding, disagreement, etc.) can ferment unnoticed for quite some time. While the organizational fire is brewing underground, it is difficult to pinpoint or even detect it. Once in the midst of a fire, executive directors will almost always say they had a sense something was wrong, an indistinct whiff of something that smelled vaguely like smoke, but ignored it because they were unable to collect concrete evidence—no visible flames. This can make you feel like you are going insane or imagining things, up until the point that it explodes and becomes a raging fire.

The spark leading to the underground fire is almost always an unhappy person who catches the ear of another person and spreads the particular grievance or dissatisfaction. Soon, you have two or more people talking amongst themselves and feeding off one another's negative energy. The fuel that keeps the fire smoldering is the attention received by the inappropriate airing of the grievance outside of the proper procedures as outlined in the organization's Grievance and Conflict Resolution Policies. The more attention received, the more the problem is legitimized and the more momentum, tension and discontent build.

Eroding Trust

As this fire is burning underground, damage is already being done. You may begin to realize that a once warm and friendly work environment has become cold, cliques have formed in the break room, former friends have ceased making eye contact, or that there seems to be a general sense of distrust. It is even common in this stage to walk into a room and immediately have everyone stop talking! At the very foundation of any non-profit, and most other organizations, is trust, and trust is exactly what is being eroded during this stage.

There is no way of telling how much damage may be done, which parts of the organization might be affected or in what way the fire may emerge.

Trust Your Instincts

Now I want to introduce you to a principle that I call "First Enlightenment". The principle of First Enlightenment teaches that you may receive an initial nudge, suspicion, intuition, concern, some hint of an alarm whispering to your spirit. This alarm needs to be acted upon. As action is taken, more enlightenment comes, but ignoring the initial alarm could completely stifle further revelation thereby leaving you open to being blindsided when the flames erupt.

As the leader of an organization, you may begin to feel that there is something wrong, perhaps by instinct or by some of the subtle signs of eroding trust. As you begin to perceive this shift in your organization, your instincts will begin to whisper to you; you must listen to them. EDs will often dismiss the feeling because they cannot "prove" something is going on, only to find out too late that their intuition was valid.

Instead, you must act. This action may be a simple move such as going to other people with a humble heart and asking, "Is everything okay? Am I missing something?" Pray and ask God to reveal the truth to you, then look for evidence or confirmation. In this stage, it is important to listen to the gentle voice of the Holy Spirit enlightening your intuition and indicating that something is amiss. When you experience this sensation, do not ignore it! God will reveal the truth to you if you ask, so pray specifically for evidence that a fire is burning in your organization.

The more you act on the First Enlightenment you receive, the more the Holy Spirit will continue to reveal.

An executive director called me expressing concern over a feeling that something was not right with her staff but she couldn't wrap her fingers around it. She was hesitant in bringing it to anyone's attention without any evidence. I encouraged her to ask God to show her what she needed to see and to take any resulting evidence to her staff to ask humbly for their input. It is almost like a scouting mission; to confirm that your instincts are correct in order to make sure you are not blind to a potentially dangerous conflict. This executive director said that she would bring it to her staff but I didn't hear back from her for several weeks.

When she called back again, she told me that the underground fire had surfaced and that it was much worse than she expected. I asked her if God had revealed any solid indicators to bring to the staff. She admitted that there were several but had postponed the conversation due to four weeks of heavy preparations for their major fundraiser. As a result, the conflict came to a head just two days before the banquet. In hindsight, the ED told me that she should have dealt with the fire as soon as she had confirmed her instincts.

Cutting Off Fuel

The good news, however, is that it is possible to stop this fire in its tracks. The solution? Act quickly and cut off the fuel supply before it spreads out of control.

I experienced this tactic firsthand as a board member of another non-profit. The organization had a very strict conflict resolution policy that included detailed procedures for each member of the organization. One day, I received a phone call from a staff member under the management of the executive director, who wanted to talk to me about her frustration with the executive director and concern about the direction of the organization. My response to her was to explain that as a board member, I was legally responsible to comply with the organization's policies and that although I was interested in hearing her concerns, I was unable to unless she followed the proper procedure as approved in our Conflict Resolution Policy. She graciously said she understood and hung up.

My next step was to contact the rest of the board to let them know that this staff may be calling them and remind them to be sure to refer her to our conflict resolution policy and procedure. She did, in fact, contact two more board members before giving up on this inappropriate method of airing her concerns. I believe that this response from the board, rather than giving the staff member a sympathetic ear and thereby undermining the executive director, prevented an underground fire that could have greatly damaged the relationship between the executive director and the board.

Humility

During this phase, it is important to take on a humble spirit as the leader of the organization. Go to your staff, volunteers and/or board members and speak honestly and truthfully. It is your responsibility as a leader to protect what God has entrusted to you and sometimes, that means asking the tough questions in order to uncover truth. The forces of darkness love to function in darkness so approaching those involved with humility and transparency may help to cast light on the situation. People will respect any leader who seeks out truth and who is willing to really listen when asking the questions. So do not react in fear, but trust that God will reveal if there is a problem.

Survival Tips

Here is some key advice to remember during stage one. First, if you are in ministry, a wise person understands that it is not a matter of IF an organizational underground fire will occur, but

WHEN. The potential will always be there as your organization is filled with daughters of Eve and sons of Adam.

Second, as I previously mentioned, most leaders facing an underground fire tell me that they could sense something was going wrong. Therefore, listen to and obey that gentle whispering of the Holy Spirit in your heart telling you that something is not right. Do not ignore the "First Enlightenment" that you receive or put it off for later. I have noticed that these fires tend to happen during the most inconvenient times possible, such as during a key transition or right before a large fundraiser. However, failure to address it immediately allows the fire to pick up momentum and may become much more devastating.

Third, seek outside counsel who has a track record of helping organizations to successfully fight underground fires. These situations can be classic examples of the proverbial dilemma of "not seeing the forest for the trees". Of the myriad breakouts I have dealt with, I honestly cannot recall even one situation when a leader was not so into the "trees" that it was not vital that s/he had outside council to bring crucial objectivity. Also, I should add here that often, it is best that the objective council reside in another community to best insure objectivity and confidentiality.

Finally, since it is possible to stop a fire in its tracks and you have God on your side, do not be afraid to act on the knowledge you have. Remind everyone of their responsibility to follow the policies and procedures on grievances adopted by the organization. As mentioned previously, humility will help root out the problem. Remember that you are looking for what is broken in the system, rather than hunting for a broken person to attack. The virtue of humility will help fight the urge to act defensively or suspiciously, both of which increase the distrust that is already growing. Underground fires are nearly always the result of a grievance which has been aired inappropriately, leading the person with the grievance to gather supporters and break up a formerly cohesive team. A defensive or suspicious reaction from the leader of the organization can result in spreading this distrust and factionalism which may be difficult or even impossible to repair.

Principle of the Power of One

One person in an organization with the wrong attitude can do great damage. In fact, my husband works with boards of directors and is constantly warning them that they are "one board member from meltdown". The same is true for volunteers and staff members—you are only as strong as your weakest team member on their worse day.

When you begin with a strong team of healthy people and you add someone who is unhealthy, something will have to give. Either the one unhealthy person leaves or is asked to leave, or the unhealthy person successfully gathers well-meaning, misguided supporters and their toxic fire will begin to spread. Ninety-nine percent of the time, these are your only options.

I'm hesitant to even mention a third possibility because its occurrence is so seldom; it may surface one percent of the time. Although extremely rare, it is possible that the unhealthy person gets healthy. The Holy Spirit has a break through, she see her need for healing, she gets help and actually follows through on the instructions of her therapist and, given enough time and work and Holy spirit intervention, she is truly healed.

It sounds wonderful, doesn't it? Who could possibly oppose healing? But there are some issues to wrestle with. You must give careful consideration to how draining this person may be, how much of your time and that of other staff is being taken away from your organization's mission to deal with this problem and how much damage to the organization is occurring while you wait for this healing

There is clearly no question that as Christians, we highly value redemption and healing but at what price to your organization? As the leader, you must decide whether helping an unhealthy staff member limp along is more important than the general health and success of the organization with which God has entrusted you. These choices will always sit right at the top of the long list of tough choices Christian leaders are required to make.

I'm emphasizing this because I have observed this more times than I can count; leaders of organizations hoping and praying that a problem employee will get better or simply go away. At the risk of sounding like Negative Nancy, I can honestly tell you that of the hundreds of similar situations that I have facilitated and observed, I only know of maybe two where the situation improved and the problem employee turned things around.

There are many reasons for this and for a good discussion of such, I would direct you once again to Dr. Henry Cloud's book, Necessary Endings for his thoughts. So, whatever the reasons, whatever your unhealthy staff member may be dealing with, the ugly reality is that people rarely change and you can't be naïve' about this. Proceed wisely.

Review the following bullet point summary often, and be alert and prepared to deal with fires as soon as you sense them. Addressing problems early can save your organization from the damage to trust that an underground fire brings.

Chapter One Summary:

Features of this stage

- Often, damage is being done without you even knowing it
- Underground fires consume the foundation of the organization - root system, trust
- Don't know where it is or where underground fires might emerge
- Can't tell how big or far reaching an underground fire may be
- Without fuel, the fire will snuff out over time

Spiritual aspects

- Holy Spirit will whisper gently- listen
- You are not alone; God will reveal the truth if you ask Him
- Remember to honor the principle of First Enlightenment
- There is nothing new under the sun – others have faced this battle too
- You can emerge out of an underground fire stronger than ever before

What to do

- Listen to your intuition and Holy Spirit
- Ask God to reveal the truth to you
- Obey the principle of first enlightenment
- Act, and act humbly but firmly
- Seek outside counsel to help you successfully navigate the issues

What not to do

- Do not act defensively
- Do not speak negatively
- Do not try to do this alone
- Do not drag out the inevitable
- Don't be naïve'; people rarely change

CHAPTER TWO

Stage Two: Flames *(Burn, Baby Burn!)*

Something's burning...

The former director of a local secular non-profit told me about his experience of an organizational underground fire. Having ignored his initial instincts, the flames came to the surface swiftly. Staff meetings were tense, his personal integrity was called into question and his best friend from work stopped talking to him altogether. Two weeks later, a few employees came to him with a letter requesting his resignation, signed by most of his staff. They contacted his superior, without his knowledge, who had listened and taken action before even speaking with the local director himself. Trust was broken with both his staff and regional leadership and eventually, he had no choice but to leave.

An underground fire in the natural world is capable of lying dormant for quite some time, slowly travelling around its subterranean world by consuming tree roots and other materials. It can, however, suddenly, and with minimal forewarning, emerge above ground once it encounters a particular point of weakness. This could be a simple thing like a structural weakness in the ground that allows oxygen to reach the flames. The fire will burst through to the surface, transitioning from a smoldering, smoky fire to faster burning flames which can quickly spread and travel in many directions.

An underground fire that has moved to the surface requires a united response from firefighters, law enforcement and the general public. It commands the immediate attention of everyone in the area and interrupts the everyday lives and basic functions of the community.

Points of Weakness

An organizational underground fire is generally fueled by the attention received for the inappropriate airing of a grievance and the bad attitude it creates in other team members. It is just a matter of time before the underground fire finds a weakness or vulnerability in the organization just like an underground fire in the natural world.

Underground fires and poor timing seem to pair up about as frequently as fish and water. It's almost spooky how flare-ups will occur at the exact worse time such as the middle of a major project or special event which commands the full attention of the executive director. Periods of transition or growth are also vulnerabilities, as the leader's attention is usually farther from day-to-day operations and team management than usual. The emergence of the fire from below ground will mean that every other project will be forced to be placed on hold. It feels like your organization is coming to a grinding halt.

Character Assassination

By this point, people are no longer talking quietly amongst themselves as they were in Stage One. Rather, they are talking openly and have banded together, perhaps approaching people in other areas of the organization. For example, a fire may spread by staff members communicating with one or more board members about their complaints. The spreading to different areas of the organization makes the issue more exposed and visible, and can also be shocking to the executive director as the attack is suddenly very personal and coming from all sides.

One challenge for most leaders is the shock of realizing that this really is happening. It is easy to become blindsided and overwhelmed by the depth, breadth and speed of the fire that recently seemed so small and indistinct. However sudden and unsettling it may be, the transition to Stage Two may make the fire easier to deal with since it is easier to address a problem that can be identified.

The most defining aspect of this stage is what I call the character assassination. This is the strangely personal nature of the attack, which moves from a grievance about an action to an all-out assault on the executive director's character. One of the biggest stumbling blocks for the ED at this point is the tendency to take things personally, which disables their response by focusing attention on personal feelings of shame, self-doubt and vulnerability. Denial is also a common response; it is hard to believe that people who are friends, co-workers and people of faith would launch such an attack. However, you must fight the urge to slip into denial and instead gear up for the spiritual battle.

Momentum

Stage Two is where those involved in fueling the fire may change from acting like foolish people to acting like evil people according to Dr. Cloud's definition. This is because there is a momentum that is in their favor, while at the same time the risk of their involvement increases dramatically. After having taken steps to bring the issue to a head, those involved must add drama to fuel the fire or else risk appearing to be in the wrong. Pride thereby becomes a driving force, though those members of the organization may not see it in themselves.

Strangely enough, those fueling the fire often come to believe they have a mandate from God to reveal what they perceive to be the truth. This is the most dangerous thing that can happen during Stage Two. This delusion may lead them to lie about the character and ethics of the executive director or other leader under attack and evolves into a personal vendetta to either remove the ED from office or to destroy his reputation. As Dr. Cloud asserts, a person who endeavors to destroy character is not acting on a mandate from God, but is actually acting in evil and sin.

One afternoon, I received a phone call from an executive director of a faith-based organization who was very upset because she just found out that a staff member had been talking to the board chairman for over a year without her knowledge. Upon further exploration, she discovered an undercurrent of frustration and distrust amongst two other staff that was being fed by the person in communication with the chair. She explained to me that within 48 hours, she went from becoming aware there was a problem to receiving a letter that was signed by four out of six of her staff demanding her resignation. The hardest thing for this ED was the fact that she had been simply unaware that any of this was going on until the underground fire surfaced and turned into a fire storm that threatened to not only destroy her but also the reputation of the organization.

Survival Tips

Despite the evil and hurtful actions of those fueling the fire, it is important to keep in mind who the real enemy is during this time. For any Christian nonprofit ministry, the true enemy is spiritual, not human. Our Enemy wants to take out leaders with the ultimate goal of shutting down the organization or rendering it ineffective in its Godly mission.

One of the key survival tips for Stage Two is to under-communicate with outsiders and to over-communicate with the board of directors. Oftentimes, you will have well-meaning individuals such as donors, supporters, pastors and other individuals outside of your organization who have heard about the conflict, contact the executive director with their concerns or advice. The last thing you want to do is to throw gas on the flames by defending yourself or giving them enough details for them to jump into the fray on one side or the other. Instead, keep your reply short and gracious, such as this: "Thank you for sharing your thoughts with me. I will take all that you have shared into prayerful consideration and bring it to the board of directors for their consideration as well." At the same time, communication with the board of directors is crucial because they are the final authority on how the issue will be handled. Remember to over-communicate with your entire board and to ask advice of your board chairman as to how he/she would want you to communicate with the board.

It is always a good idea to seek outside help and counsel during Stage Two as it is very difficult to envision a solution in the middle of the chaos. An outside confidant who understands your organization, the dynamics of organizational development and underground fires can help you respond in a calm and effective manner to your board and other members of your organization. Someone who has had experience with organizational development or crisis management will be best able to assist and teach you the firefighting techniques necessary to carry you through.

Now is also the time to start collecting the facts. That means going to people and investigating more deeply, finding out who is involved, when this started and how much damage has already been done.

Public Trust

Damage in Stage Two consists of a further breakdown in trust. Stage One begins to deteriorate trust between team members, but now both public trust and the highly important trust between ED and the board becomes affected. Public trust is compromised when the perpetrators reach out beyond the organization into the community to continue building their team of sympathetic people. As you can imagine, news of dramatic conflict at the local nonprofit can spread quickly among churches and other social circles.

Spiritual Attack

Potentially, the most painful damage at this point could be to the soul of the executive director as a result of the character assassination she falls victim to. The ED (or other organization leader) becomes the focal point of the conflict and the goal often becomes to remove her from the position.

But because organizational underground fires truly attack the character in the soul of executive directors, they will struggle with personal feelings of shame and embarrassment, or like the attack has violated their privacy and invaded their life. They will often begin to second-guess themselves at this stage, believing that they don't know what they are doing and wondering if the organization would be better served if they were to leave. In Stage Two damage, the emotional and spiritual pressure wears down organizational leaders, attacking their confidence, challenging their endurance and giving rise to negative thoughts that include a strong desire to quit.

The greatest battle here for executive directors is how they manage their thoughts and self-talk. In the Bible, II Corinthians 10:5 talks about how important it is to take every thought captive and that if any thought is not from God, we Christians must reject it as according to James 4:7. But it's very difficult during a Stage Two fire to really be discerning between what is true and what is untrue, what is from the Holy Spirit versus what comes from the forces of darkness whispering half-truths. In my opinion, the greatest damage that could occur is the loss of an executive director who was called to be the leader of the organization but who gets knocked down and knocked out.

As the fire emerges from underground in Stage Two, the executive director endures a lot of pain and emotional attack. During this phase, both the leader and the organization are put in jeopardy, and the response of the leader is crucial in determining the ultimate outcome. The key at this point is for the ED to seek counsel, rely upon God and to prepare for battle—because even greater heat is coming.

Chapter Two Summary:

Features of this stage

- Finds a weakness in the organization and exploits it
- Is out in the open now instead of people talking quietly amongst themselves
- Spreads across to different areas of the organization
- Commands immediate attention, brings other projects and priorities to a halt
- Personal vendettas and character assassinations abound

Spiritual aspects

- Denial- leader cannot slip into denial, must have a warrior's spirit
- Lack of action is tempting due to the shock and hurt of attack by co-workers and friends
- Don't take things personally – this is a spiritual attack on you and your organization
- Foolish people begin to attack the character of leadership
- Those driving the fire often feel they have a mandate from God to reveal sin

What to do

- Seek outside counsel from others who have successfully navigated such crises
- Remember who the real enemy is and the goal, which is to get leaders to quit
- Collect the facts first – who, what, when, where, why
- Over communicate with your entire board
- Take care of yourself – get plenty of sleep and exercise
- Take every thought captive – II Corinthians 10:5
- Remember that you do not get shot at unless you are flying over enemy territory

What not to do

- Defend yourself
- Over-explain to outside people – executive directors only report to their board
- Confide in staff – there is no such thing as 'off the record'
- Try to put this fire out on your own – seek outside counsel

CHAPTER THREE

Stage Three: Firefighting *(I will survive!)*

Extinguish the fire at its source...

The firefighting stage is generally the most exhausting. When I spoke to one ED during this stage, he shared with me that the hardest part for him was feeling like he was completely responsible for the mess they were in and struggling with an incredible desire to get in his car and drive away, never to return. We talked about how under great stress, the fight or flight response kicks into gear and he admitted that his flight response was in full swing. He also described the feeling that he was the only person who had ever experienced this which contributed to his feeling of unreasonable responsibility.

Then I reminded him that it was a spiritual issue and the primary goal of this fire was to get him to quit and take the organization off mission. Understanding that many others had fought similar battles before him helped him to move forward with more confidence.

In Stage Three of an underground fire in the natural world, the fire has emerged to the surface and is now spreading rapidly. It can blaze quickly out of control, forcing home evacuations and threatening lives, and requires the full attention of firefighters and rescue crews. In the beginning, the normal winds fanned the fire but at this stage, the heat becomes so intense that the fire literally "takes on a life of its own" creating its own wind, weather and humidity (lack of, that is). It is called a wildfire because it can actually become wild and crazy and completely unpredictable.

Out of Control

At this stage, an organizational fire is now dominating the organization and the life of its leader. The fire continues to gather momentum and seems to take on a life of its own, just like a natural fire. You can almost feel the heat from it as it increases. The executive director often finds herself running around putting out fires with staff, volunteers, board members, donors, and pastors as everyone is developing an opinion and taking sides.

The world of the executive director feels out of control as all scheduled goals and tasks are forced to be abandoned to give necessary attention to controlling the fire that is sweeping through the organization. Just as in a natural fire, it requires the full attention of a team of people and is exhausting and depleting.

As the fire goes outside the bounds of the original problem, volunteers become involved and more outsiders are made aware of the conflict. Despite having built a supportive network of trusted counselors, spiritual leaders and a prayer team, as well as a supportive board of directors, executive directors often report that this is the time they can feel the most isolated. It can be highly exhausting and discouraging for them to have to continually resist the sensation that they are the only one fighting the battle.

Under Attack

Understandably, this is the stage when the executive director most wants to give up. In the middle of the fight, it feels like running uphill through sand, and it is so difficult that they may not even be aware of the progress they are making. I often find myself telling EDs in stage three that it is likely to get worse before it gets better, and that is almost always the case. However, it is often right at the point when you are stretched beyond your breaking point that things begin to improve.

This stage requires a level of tenacity and endurance that most leaders have never had to possess before. They need to understand and embrace their dependence upon God and rely on His strength during this period of complete instability. Spiritual guidance and prayer partners can help keep leaders focused on God's strength, rather than trying to rely upon their own.

Relying on God will also help you to stay focused on who the real enemy is and help you to pray for the perpetrators and their change of heart, rather than allowing resentment into your heart.

One ED described her experience in this stage as an attack on her soul; "I felt like I was being wrung out, in that there was nowhere except God that was a safe place." She experienced grief-like pain and isolation along with the betrayal of close friends and co-workers. This made it difficult to persevere in fighting the fire, but being willing to confront the conflict and make the hard decision was what conquered the fire. It was two years from the beginning of the fire to its ultimate extinguishing when she was able to fire the last two staff members perpetuating the conflict. "That was the squeezing out of the final virus. You cannot get people to understand when they are in the midst of it. When it comes down to it, you have to cut your losses and move on. Ultimately", she says, "do the right thing and trust God for the outcome."

Survival Tips

There are seven actions that will significantly help you to survive this stage of an organizational fire:

1. Know Thy Enemy:

I know that I have said this before in previous chapters, but it's critical for all leaders to remember who their real enemy is. The real enemy is not human. The real enemy is the spiritual forces assigned to destroy your organization—to close you down. Know thy enemy. This spiritual enemy never sleeps, never takes days off, always hits below the belt, and will use the weakest member of your organization to light the organizational fire.

2. Do Not Throw Gas On The Fire:

There will be emails to respond to, phone calls to return, and people stopping by your office with their own opinion about what is happening, who is at fault, and what you should do about it. There is a simple rule to follow when responding to anyone who talks to you about this situation. I call this rule "thou shalt not throw gas on the fire". This is how the rule plays out; whenever you are communicating with someone about this underground fire, you do two things. The first thing you do is to watch for opportunities to restate what you have just heard people say. A really cool thing about restating is that it doesn't mean that you are agreeing with someone, it simply assures people that they have been heard. The second thing you should do is to always end the conversation by saying something like this: "Thank you for sharing your thoughts with me. I promise that I will take it into prayerful consideration and talk to the board about it".

Most people understand that they don't have the kind of power that you do as the leader or the board of the organization. What they want is to simply know that their thoughts, opinions and concerns were heard and respected.

3. Do Not Do This Alone:

Once again, I want to reinforce how important it is that the leader of the organization and the board of directors secure an experienced consultant who can help them to navigate this crisis. This consultant should be available 24/7, understand how to successfully mitigate organizational crises, be willing to help you create internal and external communications, and be equally committed to transparency in all matters.

4. The Battle For Your Mind:

Again, be very determined to guard your thoughts. Your spiritual enemy will not only attack your spirit, but your mind as well. You really are what you think.

5. Do Not Try To Fix It:

During this stage of the underground fire, I find that the leaders of the organization often begin to think if only they could say the right thing to those that are stirring up the problem so that they will have this ah-hah moment, see the error of their ways, and repent. I can't remember ever seeing that work. I think the deception is too strong and since "the right thing to say" probably doesn't exist, attempting it would likely only make matters worse.

I have also seen leaders beat themselves up inside wondering what they have done to cause such damage to their beloved organization. Refer back to number 4 above. Remember, the perpetrators, not you, made the decisions of their own free will.

6. Remove The Cancer:

Most every organizational underground fire that I have been involved with had something in common. One of the key factors that contributed to extinguishing the fire was identifying who the original primary perpetrators were in causing the fire and releasing them from the organization. The leaders of nonprofit organizations have a fiduciary duty to always act in the best interest of the corporation.

Think of it like this; if you had a cancer that was threatening your life, you would not try to reason with the cancer. Instead, you would go to an experienced doctor who has been properly educated about cancer and has a track record of helping their patients to survive this disease.

Just as cancer can destroy the human body, an organizational fire and the deception that ignited it has the potential to destroy your organization. Therefore, just as the best way to deal with cancer is to surgically remove it so the body can rebuild itself to a healthy place, the organization plagued with an underground fire must first remove those who were involved in starting the fire in the first place, as well as those who continue to feed the fire over time. I understand that this sounds harsh, but the alternative is to keep the cancer (deception) in house and watch it spread.

Get out the knife and sharpen it. Do the deed. Yes, it will be extremely painful, but you will survive and be on the road to recovery. I cannot stress this action enough.

7. Fear God More Than Sons of Adam and Daughters of Eve:

Executive directors who have survived an organizational underground fire tell me that one of the most important lessons that they learned during this time was to fear God above all others and that obedience to God was more important than pleasing the sons of Adam and daughters of

Eve. This is the principle of doing the right thing and trusting God for the outcome.

No Matter What, Never Give Up

During this period of stress and exhaustion, the temptation to just resign and go on with your life is very common and extremely tempting. In reality, this is the worst time to quit because God often uses battles such as this for His own purposes.

What may be the most powerful thing you could do at this time would be to try to gain a new perspective—a Godly, faith perspective. Ask yourself some questions that may have obvious answers but ask them anyway.

> ► Did all this drama take God by surprise? Was He blindsided by this?
> ► Is it at all possible that something good could actually come from this?
> ► Is it possible that God intended for good to result from this?
> ► Have you or someone else been praying for change of some kind in the organization?

In my Christian walk, I struggle and I think many other Christians struggle as well to fully grasp and appreciate the truth of Romans 8:28. Do we really, truly believe that "All things work together for good"? That's ALL things—ALWAYS. For GOOD. Not less bad—GOOD.

Now I have come to believe that as most Biblical promises, Rom. 8:28 is conditional. I believe that we are promised good results in any situation where our response to that situation is righteous. You know, "What Would Jesus Do?" There doesn't seem to be a qualifier on the type of situation. ALL things no matter how horrible, painful, disgusting, wretched, evil, etc. will have good results if our response is righteous.

So, in the midst of this experience, the worst you have ever endured, so gut wrenching you just want to die, before you run off and join the circus, or worse, go to work at McDonalds, look up and ask God if He might have a plan in all this. Is He trying to get the attention of leadership? Is He preparing the organization for expansion that just will not happen without some needed purification? Is He pruning the staff and/or board? Perhaps there is yet more than meets the eye and He is using all this drama and acting out to clean up an even bigger mess you aren't even aware of.

Is He revealing His character to you to grow you? Is He purifying you like He did Job?

Have you or someone else been praying for the staff or board? Just a comment here. When you pray something like, "Lord, make sure the right people are on the board (or it could be staff)," have you ever asked yourself just how you expect God to answer that? Sometimes, the only way God can move people is apply pressure, use fireworks, create drama. It can feel like He turns the organization upside down and shakes it like a pepper shaker to get the people out that need to go.

So, before you flee for your life, ask Him once more what He is doing. What is He trying to accomplish? This fire may be one reason why he called you into existence at this time in the history of mankind! YOU DON'T WANT TO MISS THIS!

The only time to quit is after you have sought God's will deeply and honestly, and you have been clearly called to move on. God has a purpose and a plan for your life so, as in all things, it is important to involve him in the process when discerning your next steps. Do not quit without seeking God's will.

Am I The Only One In This Battle? Why Do I Feel So Alone?

In this period of loneliness, remember that many have trod this path before you and most have survived within their organization. Most have, in fact, come out the other side (either within their organization or not) much stronger and more dependent on God. When you feel lonely, reach out to your support system—they are there for a reason! Do not go through this alone.

As the attack escalates and becomes more personal, those fueling the fire tend to increase in rebellion, pride and stubbornness. In extremely rare cases, these people see the error of their ways, stop the attack and repent. I must admit however, that I can count the number of times I have experienced this on one hand with fingers left over—but it is possible. Far more frequently, the perpetrators fueling the fire will end up leaving the organization, either voluntarily or involuntarily. When a fire has been able to progress to stage three, the removal of the perpetrator(s) is nearly always the only way to extinguish it.

You Can Survive

You may not feel like it when you are in the middle of an underground fire, but trust me, you can survive a stage three fire. Though you will emerge weary, you will also emerge with new-found wisdom and strength you did not have beforehand. Only at this point, when the fire has been fully extinguished, can you refocus on moving the organization forward.

Chapter Three Summary:

Features of this stage

- Fire extends and spreads
- Requires a lot of attention
- Will get worse before getting better
- Difficult to see progress

Spiritual aspects

- Feelings of isolation
- Dependence on God
- Prayer for perpetrator(s)

What to do

- Practice endurance, tenacity, prayer and discernment
- Maintain relationship with board
- Remove those from the organization who started the fire, and those who contributed to feeding the fire over time
- Take care of yourself – get enough sleep, increase exercise and focus on eating well
- Fear God more than man

- Be careful who you place your trust and confidence in

What not to do

- Don't give up!
- Do not try to reason with those who have set the fire, and those who feed the fire
- Do not try to fix people
- Do not take responsibility that is not yours
- Do not try to do this without an experienced coach or adviser

CHAPTER FOUR

Stage Four: Aftermath *(Fire always changes things)*

Didn't see that coming...

A few years ago, a leader of a Christian ministry contacted me just as the organizational underground fire was spreading to key staff and board members. Hearsay and rumors about the leader were spreading like wildfire. He asked me to come, quickly.

By the time I arrived, the attack on the leader's character was so out of control that I sent him to another town to meet with a pastoral counselor while I went to work looking for the primary source of the fire. It didn't take long before it became clear what was being said and who the two individuals were that ignited and continued to fuel the fire.

This organizational fire lasted over six months. There was a time when the fire was so intense and destructive that I wondered if the organization would survive. It was one of the worst character assignations I had witnessed to date. It was so horrible that I actually had a few conversations with the leader assuring him that God would not love him any less if he were to just declare that it was really only a bad dream and move on. But this anointed leader rose from the blackened ashes of his circumstances and with a humble heart, he took responsibility for not dealing with the issues that caused the organizational fire in the first place and created a plan for how he would do things differently in the future.

A few years later, this leader contacted me by phone and shared how he had caught the early signs of strife and had quickly doused the beginning of an underground organizational fire.

He became an inspiration to me and I often will send other leaders who are going through an organizational fire to him for encouragement.

Natural World

The aftermath of a wildfire in the natural world can be shocking and disheartening. Fires that have destroyed acres of beautiful forest or grassland leave behind a lot of devastation.

Things can be rather tense at the time a wildfire is raging, with all the eye-burning, nose-clogging smoke and the nail-biting threat of cinders that can start another fire a mile away, but when the drama is over and the fire has burned itself out, the aftermath may not be entirely negative.

Wildfires can leave a ton of fertilizer behind enriching the soil—we usually call it ash. There are evergreen trees whose cones will only open and release their seeds when burned in a fire. These trees can only reproduce in the wake of a fire. Also, in our area, there are highly valued mushrooms that only grow after a fire has swept through the area. A month or two following the inferno, people will swarm out to gather them and they can earn a fortune.

I was talking with a wheat farmer after a wildfire had burned everything all around his house—hundreds of acres of black. It burned half his wheat that would have been harvested a week later and most of a fence that surrounded several hundred acres of grazing land. I thought he would be devastated but he was very upbeat. When I asked him why, he told me that the wheat and fence were insured and when the fire scorched his grazing land, along with the grass, it also consumed all the trashy brush that had invaded over the years. While the brush was dead for good, the grass would come back, even where the brush had been. He concluded that he would be much better off with a new fence and cleaner grazing land.

I'm reminded of a phrase I heard my grandmother frequently use, "It's an ill wind that doesn't blow someone some good." Sometimes, ill wildfires can do good and so can ill organizational fires.

Parallel with Organization

It may take organizations a long time to recover from an organizational underground fire. At a minimum, it will take several months but it may be a couple of years before things are "back to normal". My observation has been, however, that within a few years, an organization that has passed through an organizational fire is likely to be stronger and more vibrant than ever, provided that they allow themselves to recover properly. Just as a wildfire purges the land and leaves behind new seeds and fertile soil, an organizational underground fire can purify and lay a foundation for future growth.

Spiritual

It is not surprising that fire plays such a significant role in the Bible as the Creator Himself is described as a "consuming fire." (Deut. 4:24; Heb. 12:29)

Fire is considered by many theologians to be a metaphor in the Bible as fire is connected with the very presence of God as evidenced in the burning bush from which God spoke to Moses (Exodus 3:2-6). Here, God even uses fire as a manifestation of himself.

In the New Testament, fire is connected with baptism such as when John the Baptist predicted that Jesus would baptize "with the Holy Spirit and with fire" and when it describes the "tongues of fire" that rested upon those gathered in the upper room when they "were filled with the Holy Spirit" (Acts 2:3-4).

In other scriptures, the anger of God is metaphorically represented by fire. Then there are the passages that speak of fire as a purifying agent capable of testing the quality of one's life and works (1 Corinthians 3:13).

Rather than being utterly destroyed, Christians can be purified, corrected, redirected and cleansed by hot painful circumstances. A fiery circumstance can bring forth a new awareness that brings healing and restoration.

Flames naturally flicker upward because it generally takes dense matter composed of different atoms and breaks them apart into simpler elements, usually gases. It is these ignited gases which produce the flame.

Fire is usually started by friction which causes a spark that produces a fire.

Fire is never neutral. It's always moving. It seeks to consume all in its path. There is the destructive fire of anger, jealousy or bitterness and the fire of passion to heal, stop evil and reach the lost.

But this one thing I know; Organizational fires change things. They force leaders to focus. They force action. They change everyone in the organization—for better or for worse.

Story

When I first met Deb for lunch, I remember thinking how petite and fine boned she was. She stood somewhere around 5'3" and I wondered if she ever had problems with people taking her seriously as the leader of one of the largest nonprofit organizations in her community.

But it wasn't long into the meal when my admiration and respect for this gentle leader began to grow. Deb told me about the organizational fire that was consuming her time, energy, and mental fortitude. Like I had heard from so many other organizational leaders before her, Deb shared how she had known for months that something was brewing in her executive team, but she just could not wrap her fingers around it. The initial discovery of the problem came at a bad time for her in that she was preparing for a major fundraising event. So she promised herself that she would circle back and get to the bottom of things when the event was over. By the time Bev was able to focus on the internal problem it had picked up so much momentum that her position in the organization was in jeopardy. Fortunately for her, the organization's board of directors entrusted to her the power to quench the internal fire. Today, Bev's advice to other CEOs is to never put off dealing with an internal fire no matter how small it may appear or how inconvenient at the time.

Survival Tips

Stage four is a period of recovery and restoration. In order to heal properly, you must take time to survey the damage and reflect on what happened, what each person's part was and what the organization should do to prevent future fires. The leader and board should assess the organization and build a strategy for restoration and future protection. The worst thing that could happen in this stage would be to pretend like the fire never happened. This would allow the organization to move forward without repairing damaged trust and would set the scene for another fire down the road.

Just as the organization must take some time to reflect and repair, so must the executive director. The same team that helped with advice and support during the fire can help to break down and comprehend past events in order to heal. Without proper recovery, a leader may continue forward with injuries that can impact their trust and leadership in the future.

Only after having healed trust can an organization move forward with new growth.

I think it is important to point out that even when the fire has been extinguished and the leader and organization have entered the aftermath or cleanup stage, it doesn't necessarily mean that the spiritual attack has ended. I have often seen situations where the organization was blasted with a devastating fire but the leadership was able to prevail and the ministry survived. The problem is that although the perpetrators may be gone, the memories are still very fresh and the leader may have some deep, painful, ugly, festering wounds to deal with.

The hurtful things that were said, the disloyalty of those thought to be loyal, the leader's underserved damaged reputation in the community, the trust that has been undermined and more can all become very fertile ground for the forces of darkness to nurture the feelings and thoughts of bitterness, ungratefulness, unforgiveness and my favorite, the "Why me, God?" questions.

This can be an extremely vulnerable time for the leader given that serious exhaustion may have set in by now which can result in even the strongest Christians feeling like they don't have the energy to resist the temptation to blame, feel sorry for themselves, become bitter and give up.

This then becomes a time to choose. If the leader chooses to listen to those dark, tempting voices and gives in to the unrighteous thoughts and feelings, then that is his choice. It is not a given, it is a choice. But there is another possible choice, most likely the tougher choice, and that is to choose to believe God and His Word and obey it.

Now is the best time to believe Paul's promise in Romans 8:28 where he states without reservation that "ALL things work together for good". This would be a perfect application of Paul's instruction in II Corinthians 10:5 to take "every thought captive to the obedience of Christ". Finally, to the hurting and exhausted, I would encourage taking James' promise literally.

"Submit therefore to God. Resist the devil and he will flee from you. Draw near to God and He will draw near to you."

James 4:7-8

Most of the leaders that I have guided through organizational underground fires have survived the attack and subsequently survived the assault on their mind after the fire was quenched. Given enough time to pass, virtually everyone that I have queried has reported that they have seen "good" results on multiple levels come as a direct result of their underground fire.

So, learn all you can about what happened to cause the flames and how you can position your organization to prevent future fires. Take care of yourself, especially while you're exhausted, by keeping close tabs on your thoughts. Also, remain hopeful, believing that the time will come when the whirlwind you just survived will make a lot more sense to you than it may right now.

Chapter Four Summary

Features of this stage:

- It will take time to recover
- Focus on any benefits that may have accompanied the fire
- The fire may have purged toxic elements from your organization
- You may be more able to grow than you were before

Spiritual aspects:

- Focus yourself and the organization on God's providence

What to do:

- Reflect, assess, make a plan
- Protect you mind—take captive of every thought
- Expect God to bring good things out of this fire

What not to do:

- Do not pretend like nothing happened and refuse to address the issue
- Do not succumb to the devil's dark thoughts and become bitter

CHAPTER FIVE

Risk Factors

A friend of mine, a former pilot during World War II, used to remind me that you only get shot at when flying over enemy territory. This has always encouraged me when I feel like I am under attack. Experiencing an underground fire is usually an indication that you are making a significant difference and the forces of darkness want to stop you by distracting you and taking you off mission.

Flying Over Enemy Territory

As a Christian leader with a mission, it is important to remember that you are flying over enemy territory and should expect to be under spiritual attack. In fact, there have been times in my life when I have questioned if I am on the right track at all when I have not experienced an attack for some time. It made me worry that I was not being effective—that I was not flying over enemy territory! Anyone in ministry can tell you, however, that the greatest danger comes not from external sources, but rather internal vulnerabilities. This can often come in the form of an underground fire.

Though many underground fires have as their source spiritual forces of darkness, we don't necessarily always have to be victims of their whims. In other words, there are steps that we can take to remove many of the opportunities that the devil is simply taking advantage of when attacking. Worse yet, most of the time, these are opportunities that we are giving to the enemy. The Apostle Paul gave some simple advice to the church at Corinth, "Don't give the devil an opportunity."

In the operating of our organizations, there are areas that are particularly vulnerable to providing the "opportunities" the devil seems to be especially gifted at taking advantage of. We will call these areas risk factors.

Here are some risk factors that may increase the likelihood of an underground fire. If your organization has any of the following predictors, you may want to pay particular attention.

Family Members

The first risk factor is having one or more staff members or volunteers that are related (by blood or marriage) to a board member. This is very common in small to mid-sized nonprofits and may work for a while depending on the organization. You may be able to continue with both the staff/volunteer and board member, so long as the potential risk has been discussed by the board and the proper risk management policies are in place. However, there are many organizations that have learned the hard way that it is far better to not allow a board member to also have a family member as a paid employee or volunteer. My observation has been that fires can be especially damaging when family members are involved, because familial relationships make it much easier to bypass the organization's grievance policies and make it more difficult to identify an underminer's behavior as inappropriate.

I saw this vulnerability in action while working with an organization where a board member had an in-law who was also a staff member reporting directly to the ED. This staff member had a strained relationship with the ED, and shared her frustration with her relative board member at a family gathering. The board member later confronted the ED during a board meeting, causing the ED to feel betrayed and undermined. As the crisis unfolded, the board member was in a position where she felt the need to defend her family member and began to talk to other board members to build her case against the ED. Although the staff member saw the damage being caused, it was too late to stop the fire and in the end, the board member decided to resign from her duties.

Of course, this could have also been prevented if the board member had followed the organization's conflict of interest policy, which prevented staff from going directly to board members for such complaints. In an ideal situation, the board member would have stopped her family member from airing her grievance and directed her to the grievance policy and procedures. In this case, I believe the responsibility lies mostly at the feet of the board member because she, as a board member, is a leader in the governing body of the organization.

Sacred Trust

The second risk factor is the relationship between the executive director and board chairman, which is what I call a sacred trust. The ED has to know that the board chairman is with her, believes in her and will back her up. As head of the governing board and head of implementing board directives, the chairman and ED together set the tone for the entire organization. A strained relationship makes it difficult for the ED to step forward with confidence of board support, and for the chairman to trust the ED to implement board directives without being micromanaged. An untrusting relationship between these key figures is an area ripe for undermining of either leader, and thus a common risk factor for an underground fire. Mutual respect is needed to repair this relationship and eliminate this risk factor.

In one organization, the role of board chairman had been filled by the same person for six years. Over those six years, a very strong relationship had developed between the chairman and the ED, and the chairman's coaching and counseling leadership style had focused on the personal development of the ED. When the chair finally stepped down, the new chairman had a very different leadership style that focused heavily on outcomes and accountability. The extreme differences in the styles of the two board chairmen were very difficult for the Executive Director to adjust to, and created the beginnings of an underground fire in which the board began to question her competency as a leader. In the end, the ED resigned due to a lack of trust with the board.

Change Management

I have observed that underground fires often occur as a high-performance organization is preparing for a significant change or period of growth. This is an area of particular vulnerability because the leadership is focused on moving forward and does not notice the early warning signs. From a spiritual perspective, it is a strategic opportunity for the forces of darkness. Evil thrives on confusion and divisiveness, which it uses to interfere with your organization's good work. Good change management, with special attention to staff, volunteers and board members who may feel threatened by changes, is critical to a smooth implementation of this stage of growth.

One organization I worked with was preparing to add a new division of services to their ministry, which required a restructuring of the entire organization and increased the pressure on raising funds. This particular leader was thrilled to be moving the ministry forward and loved this part of leadership, but concentrated so much of her time on expansion that she neglected transitional planning for staff care. When two key staff complained to her, she did not have the time to address the complaints and continued moving forward. The staff felt so strongly about it that they found an opportunity to go directly to one board member. Rather than taking the issue to the ED, this board member spread the complaint to the rest of the board, which decided to interview the key staff persons without the ED's knowledge. This greatly damaged the trust of the ED, and it took a lot of work to heal the board-ED relationship.

Overwhelmed and Overworked

The fourth risk factor is an ED who is too overwhelmed. Executive directors without the proper supportive roles and infrastructure do not have enough time to pay attention to the interpersonal and personnel problems that often ignite underground fires. If the ED is overwhelmed, exhausted or feels like s/he is never caught up, something has to change to eliminate this vulnerability. Oftentimes, hiring an assistant, re-distributing tasks and taking some personal time can help, as can the realization that constant self-sacrifice is actually not in the best interest of the organization.

An executive director I was working with had just successfully moved her organization from one level to the next, but had not increased hours for the part-time executive assistant. This left the ED with less support than she needed, and increased her stress to the point that she was experiencing mental and physical burnout. Her doctor recommended a temporary reduction in work in order to recover, but the board did not approve her request to cut down on her hours and instead, reached out to another staff member without the ED's knowledge, asking this staff person to take over some executive duties. While the board meant well in speaking with the staff member, it caused a breach in trust with the ED and unleashed an underground fire led by one of the members of the board. This is an example of how an overworked ED can cause discontent in the staff or board which leads to undermining of leadership.

Defining Roles

A lack of defined roles and structure is a fifth underground fire risk factor. Everyone in the organization should have a decent understanding of governance structure and the roles of the board, executive director and staff. Resentment and confusion can easily build when members of an organization fail to understand the specified roles of board as the governing body and executive director as implementer. This is especially true if either the board or ED steps outside of their roles and starts to meddle into the responsibilities of the other. For example, a board that steps into supervising employees and getting involved in day-to-day operations shows the entire organization their lack of trust in the ED, creating an area of vulnerability to an underground fire.

A small nonprofit asked me to help them prepare for the next level of growth. When I brought up the need for updated job descriptions, they pushed back, saying that job descriptions were limiting in such a small organization, and that not having job descriptions had worked in the past. I warned them that job descriptions were a good preventative measure to the risk factor of a lack of structure, but they insisted. Eventually, an underground fire was sparked by the lack of board understanding of staff needs, which spread to donors and church supporters.

Board Involvement

Lack of board involvement is another risk factor. Board members can sometimes be uninvolved due to their own lack of commitment, or they can be uninformed because their board chair does not keep them abreast of what is happening in the organization. Both can be risk factors for organizational crises because the board is ultimately responsible for all that happens within the organization and must act in the best interest of the organization. The board chairman's role is to facilitate decisions made by the board and should never be to take actions on their own behalf.

One particular nonprofit ministry had a board chair, one of the original founders of the organization, who had acted as chair for more than twenty years. He ran the board on a need-to-know-basis style, making all the decisions unilaterally. When I was brought on to work with them, I was forced to address this problem since he was not involving or even informing the rest of the board in many important areas. However, because this had been how things had been run for a very long time, no one really saw a need for change. Thankfully, they brought in a couple of new board members during the transition who disagreed with decisions being made without their knowledge. However, the board chair refused to adjust to a facilitating role and instead, went to churches and donors to gather support and pressure the new board members to leave. This became an underground fire that greatly impacted the organization's reputation in the community.

Finances

Financial struggle is the final risk factor for fires. Organizations that have been struggling financially for a prolonged period of time are at risk for fire due to the intense stress it places on staff who feel their positions are threatened and the stress for the ED and board to keep the organization afloat. Unhappy, underpaid staff can quickly become disgruntled and untrusting of their leadership.

I worked with one organization that had a significant failure in their annual special event. They were very dependent on this event, which usually brought in at least half of the budgeted income for the year. The revenue deficit resulted in staff being asked to take a pay cut for a few months, sparking resentment from their feeling underappreciated and disrespected. Eventually, the staff showed up to a board meeting to share their frustration, and the board responded by telling them to readjust their attitude. The underground fire that had been brewing immediately broke out into a full blown wildfire that targeted the board of directors and was very damaging to the organization.

Of course, the idea is to have the fewest risk factors possible. Using this list to assess and mitigate risk will reduce the chance of an underground fire in your organization. However, underground fires are still possible even without these risk factors. You will read more about prevention strategies in Chapter 6.

Chapter Five Summary

Flying Over Enemy Territory:

- Being effective makes you vulnerable to attack
- Forces of darkness will try to limit your efficacy by distraction and taking you off mission

Risk Factors:

- Family members of board as staff or volunteers
- Lack of trust between ED and board chairman
- Insufficient change management for staff during times of transition and growth
- ED that is overwhelmed and lacks time to address personnel issues
- Unclear or undefined roles for ED, board and staff
- Board members who are uninvolved or uninformed
- Prolonged financial stress

CHAPTER SIX

Prevention

I once worked with an executive director who was a verbal processor. She was best able to process by talking things through with other people. She was frustrated with her inability to communicate with her staff and wanted to know what she was doing wrong. We quickly discovered that the rest of the staff comprised internal processors who prefer to think through problems quietly on their own and who were constantly confused by their leader's conversations. Was she asking them to do something? Was she changing her mind about a decision? They couldn't figure her out and ended up avoiding her for fear they would be assigned yet more duties. In reality, the ED was simply processing problems and needed to talk them out. Learning about the team's differing needs and processing styles helped to improve communication and relationships.

As with most every problem, the best way to deal with an underground fire is to prevent it in the first place. Let's take a look at some prevention strategies to help organizations make sure this doesn't happen to them, or at least does not happen again.

Know Thyself (And Others)

Since organizational crises have such a large interpersonal component, relationships is a good place to begin. An organization, church or business is like a family. The best way to have a good relationship with family members is to know yourself and know one another. Knowing means understanding how each person is wired, how they relate to the world and to other people, and knowing their strengths, weaknesses and needs.

There are many great resources out there for leaders and their teams to learn about each other and how they are wired. My go-to for leaders I coach is the DISC Assessment. It is simple, easy to use, inexpensive and incredibly valuable. A second resource is Gary Chapman's The Five Love Languages, especially the corporate version, The Five Languages of Appreciation in the Workplace. Knowing how people are wired and how they best feel appreciated will go a long way towards improving communication and building fireproofed relationships.

Corporate Culture

Closely related to understanding yourself and team members is our next preventative measure. It is difficult to undermine someone you know and like, so ensuring that the corporate culture encourages positive interpersonal interaction will assist in preventing organizational fires. Any time a leader is frequently absent or lacks communication with their team, tension and distrust can take hold. It is worth the time investment to establish regular staff meetings and other interactions as a preventative measure. Furthermore, every faith-based organization should have regular prayer time set aside and should welcome prayer into day-to-day operations. Prayer helps to focus the organization's attention and purpose and welcomes God into your work. Christian leaders of secular organizations likewise need regular time with the Lord and should be praying for the rest of their team. Finally, an organization that has made their culture one of respect, where everyone is valued and input is welcomed is better protected against underground fires. Trust, the theme throughout this book, can only thrive when there is a respectful corporate environment.

An executive director I knew mentioned to me that he was not having regular all-staff meetings, nor was he consistent in meeting with those reporting directly to him. I warned him that from my observations, lack of meetings and interactions could create the type of communication vacuum from which an organizational fire could erupt. He listened and responded that he would establish regular meetings with his team. Less than six months later, he called to tell me about a fire that had emerged quickly and was now threatening his leadership position. When I asked about the staff meetings, he admitted that he had not implemented them and already regretted it because the increased communication would have prevented the fire.

The Golden Policies

In addition to these interpersonal preventatives, there are two policies the board can adopt to protect the organization: the whistleblower policy and the conflict resolution policy. These policies should be communicated regularly, at least once a year, to all staff and all board members and should be included in the new staff, volunteer and board member onboarding process.

In 2002, Congress passed the Sarbanes-Oxley act which requires publicly traded businesses to implement a whistleblower policy. Although not technically required for nonprofits, it is highly recommended by the IRS and has been basically adopted into generally accepted best practices for nonprofits. The primary purpose of this policy is to assure that any illegal or unethical conduct that is occurring within the organization will be brought to the attention of the appropriate supervisor.

A well written whistleblower policy has four components to it. Firstly, there needs to be a clear definition of what qualifies and does not qualify as a whistleblower issue, defined as any illegal, unethical or immoral act. For example, a staff member has proof that her supervisor is not following a policy of the organization that was approved by the board. This is unethical and puts the entire organization at risk. That staff person has a duty to report the violation even if it means bypassing her supervisor and speaking directly with the supervisor above her, all without any repercussion. The policy demands a duty (requirement to "blow the whistle") but then protects the whistle blower.

Secondly, there needs to be a clear description of how the whistleblower issue is to be reported and to whom to bring the problem. Then, as previously mentioned, there must also be a statement that there will be no retaliation against any whistleblower. Finally, a statement describing the consequences for those who bring frivolous or false accusations in order to dissuade those motivated by vengeance or other dishonest intentions.

The next policy that is critical to helping prevent underground fires is a clearly written conflict resolution policy that is communicated on a regular basis (at least annually) to everyone in the organization. The conflict resolution policy must be included in the onboarding of any new staff, board member or volunteer. The conflict resolution policy does not involve illegal, unethical or immoral conduct, but rather, personality conflicts, hurts, offenses, misunderstandings and disagreements in the direction that a supervisor is going.

A strong conflict resolution packet comprises three components. First is the policy itself which should cover the procedures for filing a complaint, to whom to report in a given situation, and what documentation, if any, is required.

Also included in the packet should be an interpersonal commitment agreement. This is an agreement that clearly lays out the behavioral expectations that the organization has for all staff and volunteers. It is signed by every new staff, board member and volunteer, and is also reviewed and re-signed at least annually by current employees and all others serving within the organization. Many organizations choose to review the conflict resolution policy along with the re-signing of the interpersonal commitment agreement as part of the annual performance reviews for volunteers and employees.

The third component of a conflict resolution packet is a report form template that is always used whenever policy procedures require the complaint be lodged in writing. I find it fascinating how the process of condensing the complaint down to writing causes the complainant to take the complaint a little more seriously, because in written form, the complaint appears to carry a higher accountability than just verbally complaining.

The conflict resolution policy should be a clear pathway for a staff member to seek resolution about a concern. But if the supervisor does not provide a response that satisfies the complainant, there should always be a process in place for the complaint to go to the next level.

For example, a staff person with a complaint about a decision made by the executive director shares her concerns with the ED, who explains her reasoning behind the decision. If the staff person is unsatisfied with the response and wishes to continue, she must follow the conflict resolution policy by submitting the complaint in writing to the ED who must forward it to the board chairman. The board chairman decides whether the issue should be addressed by the board or handled by the ED. This clearly defined process is important in ensuring everyone knows what is expected of them in the case of a conflict.

It is very important to remember that once policies are approved by the board of directors, the board becomes legally responsible to ensure the policy is implemented. If an organization has a conflict resolution policy (which of course they should!) it is very important that that policy is adhered to.

End of Chapter Six Summary

Interpersonal Prevention:
- Know yourself and how you are wired

- Know your team and how they are wired

- Create an open, positive corporate culture

Necessary Policies:
- Whistleblower

- Conflict Resolution

- Interpersonal Commitment Agreement

CHAPTER SEVEN

Damage

I once worked with an awesome nonprofit board of directors who fully embraced their responsibility and accountability to donors in advancing the organization's mission statement. So, when this organization was confronted with an underground fire run amok, the biggest shock for everyone was the amount of time and energy it took to deal with the internal and external fire.

Several large churches in the area contacted the executive director expressing concern and some even offered to step in to help. This of course put the leadership of the organization in an awkward place as they had to gently assure church leadership that everything was under control when in reality it was far from under control. The organizational leadership knew this, as well as the church elders.

As a result, this well-known nonprofit organization lost the support of a few churches in their community and a number of donors as they dealt with the underground fire. Losing the financial support and respect of some churches and donors was one of the hardest things for the leadership of this organization to deal with. A year later, they told me that one of the lessons that they had learned was that it was more important to do the right thing and to trust God for the outcomes than it was to worry about their reputations.

Trust and Mission Creep

I want to expand a little here on how underground fires damage organizations and interfere with their mission. In terms of the spiritual battle, the main goal of the forces of darkness is to take the organization and/or leader off of their holy mission, either by removing the leader or introducing enough hurt and confusion into the organization as to make it unable to function. Either of these outcomes can set the organization and its mission back years, and it may never fully recover.

As I mentioned in Chapter 1, trust can be compromised in all levels of the organization, even down to donors and the community. I believe that damaged trust is the most devastating result of a fire because for any kind of organization, be it a church, ministry, nonprofit or business, relationships are the glue that keep things together. Looking at nonprofits as an example, broken trust can lead to an inefficient board of directors, an executive director who can no longer lead, staff that is unwilling to carry out directives, donors that do not feel comfortable giving anymore and a community that no longer supports or seeks services from the organization. It is easy to see that broken trust means a broken organization. Trust is a difficult thing to repair and some organizations are plagued by trust issues long after the fire has been put out.

Trust begins to diminish even during the first phase of the fire, when everything is underground and the executive director may not be aware that there is a problem. Others in the organization lose trust in the leader since the person with the grievance continues to undermine, while at the same time, the leader loses trust in all who feed the attack by allowing the undermining to continue.

Another key feature of organizational underground fires is the personal attack on the executive director, board chair or other leader. Any time a person's character is brought into question, it impacts not only the heart and soul of the leader but also can deeply wound public trust. The importance of public trust cannot be overstated, especially in a church or ministry organization which is entirely funded and supported by the public and exists to be a change agent in their community. The public reputation of the nonprofit organization should always be forefront in the minds of leaders during an underground fire, because without good community support, your organization cannot serve its purpose.

The good news is that if the four stages of underground fires are clearly understood and respected and appropriate actions are taken in each stage, the organization can actually come out of a fire stronger than ever. Although in the midst of the fire, it can seem as if the organization will never recover, that is simply not the case. Almost every nonprofit that I have helped through this process has survived all four stages and nearly always come out wiser and more discerning.

A Word About Damage-doers

As long as we are talking about the damage inflicted by underground fires, let's take a moment to discuss those doing the damage. It is critical to the survival of the organization for the leadership to always remember who the real enemy is. Though it may appear to be one or more people in your organization, they are more often than not well-meaning people who have been deceived by the true Deceiver and have for a season become tools in his hands. There is not one person I have ever worked with, whether it is a board member, staff person or executive leader, who I believe woke up one morning and decided they were going to damage their organization. These people are motivated by a strong twisted conviction that they are right and that they must do whatever they can to ensure things happen their way.

I believe that those who spark underground fires nearly always do care for the organization and want it to succeed, but have been deceived and are not aware of the evil they spawn. We must remember that "the heart is more deceitful than all else and is desperately sick; who can understand it?" (Jeremiah 17:9) We human beings can convince ourselves of almost anything, no matter how well-meaning we are. The structure and accountability of a healthy organization helps to check these human tendencies and protects against the devil using our weaknesses against our mission.

End of Chapter Seven Summary

- A primary goal is to remove the leader
- Another goal is to take the entire organization off mission
- Underground fires damage trust within and without the organization

CHAPTER EIGHT

Conclusion

> "Therefore, put on the armor of God, that
> you may be able to resist on the evil day
> and, having done everything, to hold your
> ground. So stand fast with your loins girded
> in truth, clothed with righteousness as a
> breastplate, and your feet shod in readiness
> for the gospel of peace."
>
> Ephesians 6:13-15

If you are a Christian leader in any field, you can expect to experience at least one underground fire at some point in your career. Being able to identify and react properly will greatly increase your ability to fight the conflict, and the knowledge that many have gone before you victoriously can encourage and strengthen you as you encounter the emotional and spiritual onslaught. My greatest hope is that when you experience this in your organization, you can hold fast to Ephesians 6 and stand with confidence, having done all.

There are principles in the fight against organizational fires that can help protect and advance nonprofits, businesses, churches and other endeavors in other ways as well. Structure is key to ensuring the organization is able to stand tall in its mission, rather than crumpling beneath the weight of well-meaning chaos. Robust policies and regular training help keep team members united in their actions, while a warm, open work environment allows for better communication and exchange of ideas. Excellent mentorship for executive directors and other leaders can, while aiding in times of conflict, grow and strengthen a leader during calmer periods.

Finally, II Corinthians 2:11 reads, "...in order that no advantage be taken of us by Satan; *for we are not ignorant of his schemes*." I'm sure one would need to dig deep to uncover all that these eight words mean to Christians but I see two truths that seem to lie right on the surface. I think Paul is telling us that (1) we *can* be aware (the opposite of "not ignorant") of the schemes of the devil and (2) we *should* be aware of the schemes of the devil.

After over fifty years of being a Christian and more than forty years in Christian service, I am convinced that one of Satan's chief schemes, I mean the one he may use most often and possibly most effectively, is to create and take advantage of conflict amongst Christians.

I have held the belief for years now that the greatest enemy to Christian ministries is not atheists, nor the ACLU, the US Supreme Court, NOW, Satanists, the liberal media, Muslims, or any other group we could list. No, our greatest enemy is us. These groups I've listed and hundreds, maybe thousands of others can certainly be an element in Satan's resistance to Christian ministries, but I believe by far his most effective scheme is Christian servants having conflict with one another. That can tear a ministry apart in days.

I wrote this book out of a lot of frustration over what I have been seeing for years. I am frustrated over the naiveté of all of us Christians in this area of personal relationships, but what goes beyond frustration to breaking my heart is the naiveté of Christian leaders. We are grossly naive whenever we are surprised at being overtaken by an underground fire when it breaks through to the surface and goes wild.

This is one of Satan's favorite schemes—THIS IS WHAT HE DOES!! Why would we expect anything else? Dogs bark. That's in their DNA. Mosquitoes bite. You can't stop them, it's their nature. Devils divide, that's what you do if you are the devil; you spread discord among the brethren. And that is the most effective way to disable or even destroy a ministry.

So, if you are a leader of an effective Christian ministry, expect to get the attention of the forces of darkness. I will say it again, EXPECT it. Expect the attack and prepare for it. Understand they love the hidden, dark, secret places so expect it to start underground.

But expect one other thing—EXPECT TO WIN!!! If you have prepared by reducing your Risk Factors and implementing a solid Conflict Resolution Policy and a Whistleblower Policy, then you have laid a solid foundation. Add to that a corporate culture of knowing, liking, respecting and trusting each other—that means every single person on your team. Then you can, according to Eph. 6:11, "Put on the full armor of God, that you may be able to stand firm against the schemes of the devil."

"Therefore, take up the full armor of God, that you may be able to resist in the evil day, and having done everything, to stand firm."

Eph. 6:13

Know Thy Enemy...

ABOUT THE AUTHOR

Beth Chase is the CEO of Chase Advancement Inc and has over 35 years working with nonprofit organizations in organizational development, risk management, and strategic alignment. She is the host of *LifeWorked Primed* podcast and BlogTalkRadio program that airs weekly. Beth is a popular conference and workshop speaker.

Learn more about Beth at:

www.chaseadvancement.com

Do you have an Underground Fire in your organization?

Find Out now!

Download the free Assessment

Made in the USA
Monee, IL
17 March 2023

29973645R00069